BECAUSE **THEY'RE** WORTH IT

CWR

Amanda Jackson

Copyright © Amanda Jackson, 2013
Published by CWR, Waverley Abbey House, Waverley Lane,
Farnham, Surrey GU9 8EP, UK.
Registered Charity No. 294387. Registered Limited Company No. 1990308.
The right of Amanda Jackson to be identified as the author of this work has been asserted by her in accordance with the Copyright, Designs and Patents Act 1988, sections 77 and 78.
All rights reserved. No part of this publication may be reproduced, stored in a retrieval system, or transmitted, in any form or by any means, electronic, mechanical, photocopying, recording or otherwise, without the prior permission in writing of CWR.
For list of National Distributors visit www.cwr.org.uk/distributors
Unless otherwise indicated, all Scripture references are from the Holy Bible: New International Version (NIV), copyright © 1973, 1978, 1984 by the International Bible Society.
Concept development, editing, design and production by CWR
Cover images: Getty/take a pix media; sxc.hu – Nikki Brown,
Photographs: p.5 Gisela Royo, p.8 Nir Kosover, p.16 Heriberto Herrera, p.24 FoleyArt, p.32 Version Four, p.40 Nick Pye, p.46 Silvia Cosimini
Printed in England by Linney Group
ISBN: 978-1-85345-913-9

'I have a desire to see women and girls in Africa discovering purpose, unlocking potential and taking up their leadership role. I believe if women and girls discover who they are and take up their position in society it will help us to deal with some of the issues affecting women, such as poverty, violence, lack of education and low self-esteem. These studies give biblical examples and contemporary parallels of how women can relevantly contribute to the fulfilment of God's plan. I pray women will be inspired to arise and bring change to their world.'

Pastor Maureen Shana, Zimbabwe, Founder, Woman Unlimited

'Throughout time, women have shaped their world for good. This resource highlights some of these biblical, historical and contemporary daughters of God whose courage, tenacity, and compassion have made a world of difference. Delving into this inspirational material will challenge you to be the women whose ardent advocacy offers hope and restores community life, so that women and girls worldwide may fulfil their destiny.'

Marijke Hoek, co-editor *Micah's Challenge: The Church's Responsibility to the Global Poor*

'It's sadly true that women and girls in many parts of our world live in poverty – without dignity or opportunity. Who better than women to reach out to other women – to advocate for hope, restoration and justice. These studies help us to see the challenges and inspire us to see how we can be part of the solution.'

Darlene Zschech, Pastor, Hope Unlimited Church, worship leader and co-founder of Hope Global

My appreciation goes to Shunu Chowdhury

and Marijke Hoek for their insights and wise advice

on the content of these studies.

Contents

May we be dangerous women.
May we be women who acknowledge our power to change,
and grow, and be radically alive for God.
May we be healers of wounds and righters of wrongs.
Lynne Hybels[1]

Introduction

The studies in this booklet are designed to give you a picture of what women, inspired by faith, can do to tackle life's big issues; how we can overcome the injustice that many millions of women and girls face.

Women have always faithfully served others. But we have not often seen ourselves as influential. Or perhaps we are happy to accept new challenges, we just don't know where to start.

So what could we do if we captured God's vision of women relating to women around the world on big social, economic and spiritual issues?

There are 900 million women and girls around the world denied opportunity and hope by poverty.[2] Women own only 1% of the world's wealth.[3] Half a billion cannot read or write.[4]

What if we could be women for 'such a time as this' – like Esther who was called to use her influence to rescue her people (see Esth. 4:14) – a time to speak out about the suffering of women and girls around the world?

We have a unique opportunity right now. In 2000, 189 nations of the world promised through the Millennium Development Goals to halve extreme poverty in a generation – and we could help to deliver that promise. We could be women for just such a time – to address the physical, social and spiritual roots of poverty.

And what if it was something fun and relevant to all the other stuff we do in our busy lives?

There are four studies in this booklet, each with a 'Bible Foundation' section, 'Vital to Know' statistics and 'Lives to Inspire' containing stories about women. There are also suggestions on books and contemporary movies to spark discussion – as well as plenty of ideas for action.

And let me be honest – I do want to see action. I want to see a movement of women which will bring change for women and girls in this generation so that one half of God's humanity can be all that our Creator God intended.

These studies are not about us affirming each other as beautiful and worthy (although we are): more than that, we're going to explore being ordinary women doing extraordinary things – to bring God's hope for women down our road and across the world.

Amanda Jackson, 2012

NOTES

1 Lynne Hybels, *Nice Girls Don't Change the World* (Zondervan: 2006) p.91.

2 UNIFEM quotes that 70% of the world's poorest people are women. 1.4 billion live on less than $1.25 a day, the accepted definition of extreme poverty. (70% of 1.4 billion = 980,000,000.) See http://www.unifem.org/gender_issues/women_poverty_economics/

3 World Bank World Development Report 2012, reported in Huffington Post, 20 August 2012. See http://www.huffingtonpost.com/2011/09/19women-make-only-1-percent-wealth_n_969439.html

4 The CIA World Factbook 2012 estimates that there are 785 million illiterate adults and two-thirds are women, ie 590 million. See http://www.cia.gov/library/publications/the-world-factbook/geos/xx.html

(1) God's power in our weakness
(2) Jesus's attitude to women.

STUDY ONE:

Faithful servants

Don't be threatened by this. Most of the women we talk about had no idea how influential they were.

THE BIBLE AND HISTORY GIVE US MANY EXAMPLES OF WOMEN WHO PRACTISE THEIR FAITH OVER A LIFETIME, WHO HUMBLY ACKNOWLEDGE THEIR NEED OF GOD AND WHO RESPOND TO GOD'S CALL TO CHALLENGE UNFAIRNESS AND INJUSTICE.

Their humility is not a sign of weakness – it is a question of acknowledging the way the world operates and yet overcoming that view, because God has a work for them. Women throughout history have often been seen as weak, but, as we know from Scripture, God's strength is at work in human weakness (Rom. 8:26–27; 2 Cor. 12:7–10).

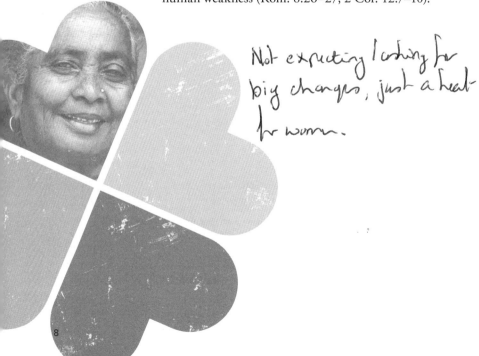

Not expecting / asking for big changes, just a heart for women.

BIBLE FOUNDATION

The Bible repeatedly affirms women who found ways to serve faithfully in times when women were not treated as equals. At the bottom of the social pile in Bible times were women without a man to protect them – widows and single women, and lower again, prostitutes.

Jesus showed the importance of supporting women on the edge of society throughout His ministry. The Gospel of Luke alone contains numerous references to women being affirmed by their special encounters with Jesus (see Luke 2:36–38; 4:26; 7:11–15,37–50; 8:43–48; 10:38–42; 13:10–17; 18:1–5; 20:46–47; 21:1–4).

BREAKOUT Q

- Consider these references in Luke.
- What evidence do we see of women being faithful?
- How would you sum up Jesus' attitude towards women?

VITAL TO KNOW

Almost four million girls and women 'go missing' each year in developing countries: they are aborted, left to die after birth, neglected in childhood and confronted with pregnancy when their bodies are ill-equipped to cope.[1]

In many places, cultural tradition and poverty mean that families value boy babies more than girls. In places like China and India, female infanticide, though illegal, is widely practised. For every 1,000 boy babies in rural India, there are only 929 girls – girls in Hindu families are often aborted or left to die.[2] In China the one-child policy (which has been relaxed in recent years especially in farming communities) has strengthened a traditional tendency to favour the boy child. Sadly, female infanticide is overwhelmingly a crime committed by women.

In the next two decades 30 to 50 million men in China will not be able to find wives.[3] There is a growing slave trade in bringing girls from places like Vietnam to fill the need for wives.

In addition, female children in many poor places are more likely to be neglected and denied proper medical care or taken to the doctor later than their brothers. And 39,000 baby girls die annually in China because they don't get the same medical care as boys.[4] The low status and vulnerability of women can also be seen in the treatment of widows in some parts of the world. It is not merely that widows have lost their husbands, the main breadwinner and supporter of their children, but widowhood itself consigns them to the very margins of society. They may be deprived of property, accused of witchcraft or forced to stay indoors.

In some countries over 50% of all adult women are widows, especially in conflict zones. For example, there are estimated to be over 700,000 war widows in Iraq.[5]

To find out more, visit: www.oneworld.org and www.gendercide.org

BREAKOUT Q

- What can Christian women do to affirm the status of girls and women on the margins of society?

LIVES TO INSPIRE

Nothing short of the Holy Spirit can really help forward the cause of righteousness on earth.

Elizabeth Gurney Fry (1780–1845)

Naomi, the mother-in-law of Ruth lost her husband and both her sons in a strange land and she felt her life was over.

Remember how Naomi changed her name to Mara, meaning 'bitter'? But she has an abiding sense of God's provision despite her hardships. When Boaz favours Ruth whilst she is gleaning in his field, Naomi recognises God's kindness. She encourages Ruth and we all know there is a happy ending: Ruth and Boaz have a son and Naomi becomes a grandmother. She reverts to her old name meaning 'pleasant'.

You can read Naomi's story in the book of Ruth.

I met **Sarah**, a Zambian grandmother, in a village two hours' drive from Lusaka. At forty-four, with eight children of her own, she had taken on responsibility for four extra children who were AIDS orphans. She had also inspired her village to dig two wells so that women and girls were saved from a 4km trek to draw dirty water. She was a stately and beautiful woman who was not aware that she was an inspiration to the whole village until they urged her to stand for local election.

When I met her, Sarah was a respected leader, making sure the wells operated properly and taking village concerns to council. She was working to start vegetable gardens near the wells so that run-off could be channelled onto the garden plants. She was also fierce in her efforts to collect the small contributions from each family that would keep the well in good working order.

Elizabeth Fry wrote in her diary when she was seventeen in 1797, 'I must not give way to luxury; I must not be idle in mind, I must try to give way to every good feeling, and overcome every bad ...'[6]

After thirty years working with women in prison – reforming conditions in the UK and Europe, she wrote, 'Since my heart was touched at seventeen years old, I believe I never have awakened from sleep, in sickness or in health, by day or by night, without my first waking thought being how best I might serve my Lord.'[7]

What happened in those years between seventeen and her death aged sixty-five is an inspiration.

Yet, when she was a young mother in early nineteenth-century London, she confided to her diary that she thought her life had 'little purpose'.[8] For many years her principal occupation was as mother to eleven children. She was not *always* a social reformer. She and her husband had to rebuild their lives and reputation during middle age when his bank collapsed. But through all these experiences, Elizabeth was ready to be used by God.

When a friend took her to Newgate women's prison for the first time, Fry was in her early thirties. She simply wanted to offer practical help – warm clothes and bedding. But once she saw the conditions of the children and understood more about the prison system, she began to advocate for change.

Six years later, she was asked to testify before Parliament about prison conditions and contributed to a growing reform movement that saw prisons become more humane places. She also pioneered nursing training, free libraries and education for poor children. What a woman!

I'm taken with the fact that pictures in history books of women like Elizabeth Fry or Florence Nightingale show them as demure elderly creatures (with funny mobcaps!). We forget that they were teenagers, young mums and capable forty-somethings. Fry was in her thirties before she found the purpose that would set her passion alight, and she was still speaking up for prison reform in her sixties.

Read more about Elizabeth Fry at: http://www.quakerinfo.com/fry.shtml

BREAKOUT Q

- How do these three stories inspire us?

- How did each of these women deal with injustice?
- Could God be calling you and your group to be women faithfully tackling injustice? Or has He already called you? Why not share your stories on Facebook, w2wglobal to encourage others?

PRAYER

Summarise the things that have inspired you in the lives of Naomi, Sarah and Elizabeth Fry. Pray for each other and ask God to show you His big picture for your life.

ACTION

So many women I know have important jobs in HR, teaching, law and health. They have families to run, they find time to lead homegroups, do some extra study or even open their homes to foster kids. I have also been privileged to work with many young female graduates who, fresh from university, bright, creative and idealistic, want to work as campaigners to make the world a more just, more godly place.

Yet most of these women do not see themselves as leaders and they often receive little recognition in Christian organisations or the local church. I find that frustrating but it's also a challenge to all of us to encourage one another to be all that we can be and to take the lead in addressing the wrongs we see.

BREAKOUT Q

- Is it right or wrong to celebrate the stereotypical image of women humbly serving others?
- Think of a way you can bless and affirm a woman in your life who displays humble faithfulness and a passion to serve.
- Think of a way you can bless and affirm a woman in your life who doesn't quite fit that mould!

MOVIE EXTRA

The Blind Side is a film about a privileged white Christian family in the States who 'adopt' a homeless black teenager, Michael Oher, with amazing football potential. Watch the film together or with friends/family during the week.

Based on a true story about the Tuohy family, the film was inspired by the book *The Blind Side: Evolution of a Game* by Michael Lewis. Here is an extract from the article he wrote prior to the book's publication:

'Leigh Anne Tuohy grew up with a firm set of beliefs about black people ... "I was raised in a very racist household," she says. Yet by the time Michael Oher arrived at Briarcrest, Leigh Anne Tuohy didn't see anything odd or even awkward in taking him in hand ... She could not say exactly how such a change happened.

"This child was new; he had no clothes; he had no warm place to stay over Thanksgiving. For Lord's sake, he was walking to school in the snow in shorts …" Of course she took him out and bought him some clothes. It struck others as perhaps a bit aggressively philanthropic; for Leigh Anne, clothing a child was just what you did if you had the resources. "God gives people money to see how you're going to handle it," she says. And she intended to prove she knew how to handle it.'[9]

BREAKOUT Q

- In the film the character Michael Oher says that we should try to have honour and courage and pray for others to have some too. Did you like the film's portrayal of Leigh Anne? Do you think she has honour and courage? Is Michael portrayed in this way?
- Is the film too saccharine about faith?
- Does the film address injustice or just philanthropy?
- Would you do what Leigh Anne did?
- If we have education and money, do you think we have an extra responsibility to speak out against injustice?

NOTES

1 See http://www.genercide.org/case_infanticide.html
2 *Ibid.*
3 Reported in *The Guardian*, 2 September 2011. See http://www.guardian.co.uk/world/2011/sep/02/china-village-of-bachelors
4 Blog by Carolyn McCulley, see http://www.truewoman.com/?id=825
5 For United Nations Millennium Campaign estimate, 2010, see http://www.un-ngls.org/spip.php?page=amdg10&id_article=2616. See also Oxfam statistics on Iraq's widows quoted by CNN online, 2009 at http://articles.cnn.com/2009-03-07/world/iraq.women_1_survey-widows-iraq?_s=PM:WORLD
6 Diary entry quoted in Mrs E.R. Pitman's 1884 biography of Elizabeth Fry. See http://www.gutenberg.org/files/16606/16606-h/16606-h.htm#CHAPTER_II
7 *Ibid.*
8 *Ibid.*
9 Michael Lewis, 'The Ballad of Big Mike', *NY Times magazine*, 24 September 2006. See http://www.nytimes.com/2006/09/24/magazine/24football.html?pagewanted=all

Gods attitude to the poor
Jesus attitude to women

STUDY 2: ~~Outsiders~~ Challenging facts.

Outsiders with influence

WOMEN ARE OFTEN OUTSIDERS ON THE FRINGES OF SOCIETY BUT THEY UNDERSTAND GOD'S HEART FOR THE POOR AND POWERLESS.

We can feel like outsiders - part-time work, locum work, lack of confidence

Women sharing and working together can open up new ways of addressing injustice precisely because they don't have access to traditional power structures. God can use outsiders.

BREAKOUT Q

- What importance do women and 'women's issues' have in your local church?
- Do women lead? Are women supported? Do girls have positive role models of women in leadership?
- Do these things matter?
- What could change for women in your local church and how could you change it?

BIBLE FOUNDATION

The Bible communicates a consistent message of justice for the oppressed and disadvantaged, who are often described simply as 'widows and orphans' or 'aliens and strangers' (see Deut. 10:18; 24:19–21; Psa. 146:9; Zech. 7:9–10). Living in a male-dominated society, Jesus frequently ministered to women and included women in His ministry, teaching them, training them and enjoying their friendship. Likewise, Paul, much misrepresented when it comes to women, declared that in the new kingdom of Christ, there was to be no difference between men and women; he endorsed women as deacons and prophets (see Gal. 3:28; Rom. 16:1). In Jesus' day women were not allowed to testify in a court of law and it is also interesting to note that in the great Temple at Jerusalem women were limited to one outer court which was five steps below the court for men.[1] A Rabbinical saying about women was, 'They are greedy at their food, eager to gossip, lazy and jealous.'[2] This indicates a deplorable attitude toward women and hints at a lack of self-respect among the women themselves.

Yet, in spite of this prevailing attitude, Jesus clearly treated women and men as equals, a radical move that subverted Jewish custom.

In Matthew 28:1–7, after Jesus' resurrection, Mary Magdalene and the other Mary are given the responsibility to tell the good news of the resurrection to the disciples. This is reinforced by Jesus' appearance to the two women. Dorothy Sayers, the novelist and religious writer said about Jesus: 'They [women] had never known a man like this Man – there never has been such another. A prophet and teacher who never nagged at them, never flattered or coaxed or patronized … who took their questions and arguments seriously; who never mapped out their sphere for them, never urged them to be feminine or jeered at them for being female; who had no axe to grind and no uneasy male dignity to defend; who took them as he found them and was completely unselfconscious.'[3]

BREAKOUT Q

Josh 2:1, 2-6, 8-10, 12, 13-14
let down ē rope, tied scarlet ribbon a window & was saved.

- Take a look at the Old Testament story of Rahab in Joshua 2 and Hebrews 11:31.
- What strikes you about this story?
- How does Rahab go about advocating for herself and her family?

VITAL TO KNOW

Lives of Girls and Women in 10 Facts[4]

1 There are 900 million women and girls around the world denied opportunity and hope by poverty.

2 Women own only 1% of the world's wealth.

3 Women produce up to 80% of food in developing countries, but are likely to be unpaid, and are often denied the right to own land.

4 Two-thirds of the 137 million illiterate young people in the world are women.

5 Each year, 295,000 women die from pregnancy-related causes, 99% of them in developing countries. Two-thirds of pregnant women in the poorest countries give birth without skilled help.

6 More than 140 million girls and women alive today have suffered female genital mutilation. In Africa, three million girls a year risk mutilation.

7 Violence against women aged fifteen to forty-four causes more death and disability worldwide than cancer.

8 There are three million girls and women worldwide who are enslaved in the sex trade – victims of violence and intimidation, with no rights.

9 Estimates of the number of victims of trafficking range from 500,000 to two million per year. The majority are female and poor.

10 Only 19% of parliamentarians globally are women. Fifty countries have fewer than 10% representation by women.

BREAKOUT Q

- Which statistics in the list surprise you? Which make you angry?
- In 2000, nations of the world agreed on eight goals to overcome extreme poverty by 2015.[5] Called the Millennium Development Goals (MDGs), three are specifically about women and girls – Goal 3 sets targets for gender equality, Goal 4 aims to reduce child mortality by half and Goal 5 aims to reduce maternal deaths by three-quarters. All nations, rich and poor, have targets to make the goals a reality.
- Can you see ways that you could help these goals to be met?

LIVES TO INSPIRE

We are for life and creation, and we are against war and destruction, and in our rage, we screamed that the violence had to stop. But we also began to do something about it besides shouting.

Máiread Corrigan Maguire and Betty Williams

(Nobel Peace Prize acceptance speech, 1977)

The Hebrew midwives, **Shiphrah and Puah** feature in the story of Moses. As outsiders, they risked their lives by defying Pharaoh's cruel decree to kill all male Jewish babies. Even though they were slaves themselves and they had been taken into the presence of Pharaoh, the Bible says, '[They] feared God and did not do what the king of Egypt had told them to do ...' (Exod. 1:17). Instead they stood in solidarity alongside the women giving birth and saved the lives of many baby boys, one of whom was Moses.

When Pharaoh realises that his command has not been carried out, he confronts Shiphrah and Puah. Their excuse is creative – Hebrew women have easy births and their babies are born before the midwives arrive!

God also has a blessing for the women – because they had faith in God, 'God was kind to the midwives and the [Hebrew] people ... became even more numerous' (Exod. 1:20). Read the full story about Shiphrah and Puah in Exodus 1:15–22.

Máiread Corrigan Maguire was born into a poor Catholic family in Belfast, Northern Ireland. She became a part of the peace movement in 1976 when two of her nephews and a niece were killed on a Belfast street by the getaway car of a gunman from the Provisional IRA. The driver of the out-of-control car had been shot dead by British soldiers.

You can imagine the tension on the streets following the deaths. Everyone could point a finger – at the IRA, at the British, at the Protestant militia. The community, outraged by the needless deaths of these children, came into the streets to mourn. Corrigan, in her thirties, joined with Betty Williams who witnessed the accident, and a journalist Ciaran McKeown, to organise weekly peace marches and demonstrations. Initially fifty women marched for peace, pushing baby carriages, and that evening on the TV news, Mairead Corrigan became the spokesperson, pleading for an end to violence.

As women outside the tangle of power structures in Northern Ireland during the Troubles, you would think they had no voice. But they persevered. Over four months there were twenty-six peace marches, and more than half a million people attended rallies in Belfast and across the UK. The women also began peacemaking programmes – one of their main ideas was to integrate schools, recreation centres and residential areas. Corrigan visited the USA, where much funding for the IRA came from, to present the case for non-violence.

Corrigan and Williams received the Nobel Peace Prize the following year. Peace did not come to Northern Ireland for another twenty-two years but the campaign by the women made violence less acceptable and peace a possibility.

BREAKOUT Q

- What strikes you about these women?
- How did they use their outsider status to be effective advocates?
- Máiread Corrigan has been criticised for her 'emotive' plea for peace which was not backed by a concrete plan for change. If this is true, what could she have done differently?

PRAYER

Pray for women to speak out on behalf of the poor and marginalised.

Pray for people who work in maternal health. Thank God for their desire to serve, and ask Him to raise up more men and women who want to stop deaths in pregnancy and childbirth.

ACTION

Christians rightly care about family issues: Western churches have lots of programmes for children and teens. We are concerned about the sexualisation of girls, body image, boys doing well at school, dating, values in education and much else besides.

But how much energy do we give to family issues facing *global* church communities, most of which are poor?

What do you think a church in an informal settlement (ie a slum) in Nairobi might say about the issues they face?

BREAKOUT Q

- Check out what your group/church does about the reality of poverty.
- What is positive about your list?
- What is missing?
- Name one commitment your group can make to bring change for women and girls in poverty.

MOVIE EXTRA

Jane Eyre tells the story of orphaned Jane – intelligent, independently minded, faith filled – searching for fulfilment and love in the constraints of nineteenth-century society. Christian hypocrisy is seen in the figure of the cleric Mr Brocklehurst who runs a charity school, and severe Christian self-discipline is personified in St John Rivers. Despite all the hardships and setbacks, Jane blossoms into a caring, patient and forgiving woman.

Throughout, there is a strong theme of service and self-control.

The heroine, Jane, is an outsider because she is poor and plain. She experiences injustice yet overcomes her narrow background and champions the cause of other girls who are victimised by society – her saintly schoolmate, Helen, her illegitimate charge, Adele, and the Rivers sisters, who take her in when she is desperate.

In the book, Jane remarks upon the distinction society makes between the sexes:

'Women are supposed to be very calm generally: but women feel just as men feel; they need exercise for their faculties, and a field for their efforts as much as their brothers do; they suffer from too rigid a restraint, too absolute a stagnation, precisely as men would suffer; and it is narrow-minded in their more privileged fellow-creatures to say that they ought to confine themselves to making puddings and knitting stockings, to playing on the piano and embroidering bags.'[6]

BREAKOUT Q

- How are 'Christians' portrayed in the film?
- What does the film say about poverty, women and power in nineteenth-century England?
- Is that portrayal relevant today?

NOTES

1 F.F. Bruce, *Commentary on 1 and 2 Corinthians* (The Attic Press, 1971) p.140.

2 From article by Leonard Swidler, 'Jesus was a Feminist', http://www.godswordtowomen.org/feminist.htm

3 From essay by Dorothy L. Sayers, 'Are Women Human?', 1938, quoted on http://www.journeywithjesus.net/BookNotes/Dorothy_Sayers_Are_Women_Human.shtml

4 1. UNIFEM quotes that 70% of the world's poorest people are women. 1.4 billion live on less than $1.25 a day, the accepted definition of extreme poverty. See http://www.unifem.org/gender_issues/women_poverty_economics/
2. World Bank World Development Report 2012, reported in Huffington Post, 20 August 2012. See http://www.huffingtonpost.com/2011/09/19/women-make-only-1-percent-wealth_n_969439.html
3. See the website of the United Nations Food and Agriculture Organisation, http://www.fao.org/sd/fsdirect/fbdirect/FSP001.htm
4. UNESCO, 2010, http://www.uis.unesco.org/FactSheets/Documents/Fact_Sheet_2010_Lit_EN.pdf
5. World Health Organisation, maternal mortality fact sheet, 2012, http://www.who.int/mediacentre/factsheets/fs348/en/index.html
6. WHO female genital mutilation fact sheet, 2012, http://www.who.int/mediacentre/factsheets/fs241/en/
7. Say No To Violence fact sheet, http://saynotoviolence.org/issue/facts-and-figures
8. Nicholas Kristof and Sheryl WuDunn, *Half the Sky, How to Change the World* (Virago, 2010) p.119.
9. April Rieger, 'Missing the Mark: Why the Trafficking Victims Protection Act fails to protect sex trafficking victims in the United States', in *Harvard Journal of Law and Gender*, Vol 30, 2007, p.231, http://www.law.harvard.edu/students/orgs/jlg/vol301/rieger.pdf
10. House of Commons Library, UK, International Women's Day 2012, Background and Statistics, p.4.

5 For a description of each goal, go to www.un.org/millenniumgoals

6 Remark by Jane in Charlotte Bronte, *Jane Eyre* (Penguin English Library, 2012 edition) p.129.

STUDY 3:

Sisters against poverty

WOMEN ARE ALLOWED TO BE BOTH LEFT (LOGICAL) AND RIGHT (CREATIVE) BRAIN-ORIENTED.

The language of women is about relationships, families and communities but, combined with emotional intelligence, we also have rational, practical insights. This double whammy of skills can be effectively used to overcome the injustice that affects many millions of women.

However, poverty robs women of relationships, friendship, relaxation and space in which to pass on wisdom. Women simply do not have time for more than surviving – collecting water, preparing food, looking after children, labouring for income.

Ironically, wealth and success can also rob us of time and friendship because of our work and family obligations.

Christian women should surely be modelling positive relationships that support a balanced use of time and energy.

BREAKOUT Q

- What things could stand in the way of women working to bring hope and justice to other women?
- Are our female friendships always strong?
- If we are pro-women, does that make us anti-men?

BIBLE FOUNDATION

The women who rescued Moses as a baby were an unlikely alliance from the very highest and lowest social classes in Egypt.

The daughter of Pharaoh ignored her own father's directive and risked his wrath by taking in a Jewish baby she found in the river. She later adopted him as her own son.

Moses' older sister **Miriam**, from the Jewish slave class, was bold enough to approach the Egyptian princess to tell her that she knew of a wet nurse who could feed the baby. This nurse was of course Moses' real mother.

Moses' mother, also a slave, hid her baby for three months to defy the ruling of Pharaoh that all Jewish boys be killed. She nursed her son but then had to hand him back to Pharaoh's daughter.

I long to know the motives and feelings of the women in this story, but even the simple narrative (found in Exod. 2:1–10) demonstrates how women are empathetic to the needs of family and can cross huge social divides to take action against injustice. They discover their destiny outside the social structures in an ancient form of sorority or female support network.

The daughters of Zelophehad from the tribe of Manasseh are five single women left without an inheritance when their father dies. According to the Law, his land would pass to the nearest male relative – leaving the women destitute. In reaction to this law, the sisters boldly pursue a claim before Moses and all the Jewish leaders to change it. Their argument is clever – appealing on behalf of their father's name rather than their own rights – and direct. They go straight to the national leader, Moses. You can read the outcome of their advocacy in Numbers 27.

BREAKOUT Q

- How do these women overcome injustice?

- Neither story actually mentions prayer or faith but how are God's values demonstrated?

VITAL TO KNOW

The happiest day in most mothers' lives is also the most dangerous one. The risk of death in pregnancy and childbirth remains as high as 1 in 50 in the poorest parts of the world.[1] Millions of these women and girls go to church and pray for a healthy birth but have little power to improve their life chances.

A woman dies every 80 seconds in the developing world because of childbirth complications.[2] Of all the Millennium Development Goals, Goal 5, the one that aims to address maternal deaths, is at greatest risk of failure. In some countries like Zimbabwe and Afghanistan, the picture is actually worse than it was ten years ago. At a time that should be a joyous celebration of new life, the dangers for mother and child are great.

Most risks are easily preventable. Educating girls about reproduction so they know what to expect, making sure surroundings are clean, ensuring the mother and child keep hydrated and having early access to help if there are complications – can all help to reduce risks.

Other risks are associated with culture and tradition. If girls marry in their teens and have babies before their bodies are fully developed, pregnancy and childbirth are dangerous. The cruel practice of genital mutilation means women face severe bleeding and pain in childbirth. Sadly, girls and women may not have the power to plan their pregnancies nor the independence to seek medical help when needed.

Maternal mortality is a rare phenomenon in the developed world (a 1 in 3,800 chance[3]) because free obstetric care is almost universally available. Indeed some midwives feel there is too much intervention! But maternal mortality has not been given high political and spending priority in many developing nations because women's status is low in the countries where maternal mortality is highest. It is a pervasive neglect of a woman's right to life.

The health of mothers also has great implications for their children (MDG-4). When women die in childbirth, babies are often undelivered. Even if women survive very difficult labour or other complications, babies are often stillborn. The survival chances of orphaned babies are reduced throughout infancy.

There are other potential consequences of maternal death. Children may stop going to school because of increased household chores after a mother's death and this may be particularly true for girls. Family disintegration following a mother's death is likely and increases children's vulnerability overall.

For more information on this topic, see http://www.micahchallenge.org/about-us/mdgs/mdg5-maternal-health

BREAKOUT Q

- If you are a mother, what was your experience of childbirth?
- What could you do to improve the prospects for millions of women who face childbirth with trepidation?

LIVES TO INSPIRE

Wars, wars, wars. War deprives Congo of 60% of its revenue from resources, resources that benefit foreign powers and lucrative business interests. Sexual violence is rampant. [But] there is a hopeful sign. Because of lobbying, people are becoming aware of this problem and the advocacy campaign has been bearing fruit.

Lyn Lusi *(speaking to the Lowy Institute, Australia, 2009)*

Leymah Gbowee from Liberia is forty years old. Since she was a teenager, her country has suffered brutal civil war which killed around 250,000. About nine years ago, she decided to do something about the violence, rape and death. In 2003, she led women from all ethnic and faith groups in fasting, praying and a public protest calling for peace.

Liberia's second civil war, 1999–2003, brought an unimaginable level of violence to a country still recovering from its first civil war (1989–96). And much of that violence was directed at women: rape and brutality were used as weapons in the war.

Sick of the violence, Leymah Gbowee, then a social worker and single mother of four, helped to organise a women's peace movement. Dressed in white, thousands of women staged pray-ins and non-violent protests demanding reconciliation and resumption of high-level peace talks.

As part of the movement, Gbowee organised thousands of women to protest in the capital, Monrovia, helping to push Charles Taylor – who is now on trial for war crimes – out of power and end the conflict. She also encouraged women to take part in elections and even suggested Liberian women go on a sex strike in a bid to bring the warring men to their senses.

Now that the conflict has ended, Gbowee has written a book, *Mighty Be Our Powers: How Sisterhood, Prayer, and Sex Changed a Nation at War*. She is also involved in peace work in other parts of Africa.

Leymah Gbowee was one of three women awarded the Nobel Peace Prize in 2011.[4]

In another conflict zone in Africa, in Goma in the Democratic Republic of the Congo (DR Congo), a hospital has been established to restore hope to women and girls, many of whom are victims of violence and rape. Staff there tend to 400 rape victims a month, most of them suffering with fistula.

Almost unknown in the developed world, fistula is all too common a condition where women are victims of rape, where girls with immature bodies fall pregnant and where women suffer prolonged labour. It is a hole between the birth passage and bladder which means that the woman will constantly leak urine. This leads to infection, loss of dignity, social isolation and rejection by family. Yet in most cases, the hole could be mended and hope restored. That is what the hospital in Goma does with outstanding success.

The co-founder of the hospital was **Lyn Lusi**, an Englishwoman married to Kasereka, the surgeon whose faith-filled vision it was to heal the lives of girls and women.

I met Lyn Lusi in Australia several years ago, when we arranged for her to meet with senior politicians to tell them about the human face of poverty and the work of her charity. She had a disarming smile and sweet manner but also a firm resolve to be a voice for the women she served. She was committed to healing women physically, emotionally and spiritually and the hospital provides all sorts of programmes to help women who cannot return home, to teach girls and women about health issues, to encourage conflict resolution in villages and to train women as leaders. Lyn Lusi died in 2012 but the work of her charity, HEAL Africa, continues.[5]

BREAKOUT Q

- The methods of modern conflict can mean that many civilians are caught up in the violence. How do you respond to the stories from Liberia and DR Congo? Sad & a bit helpless

PRAYER

Pray for women and girls who are caught up in the terror of conflict. Pray against warlords, corrupt leaders and foreign interests (most of them 'reputable' companies) that destroy lives.

ACTION

Women can advocate for women and girls caught in the desperate hopelessness of violence.

We can learn about the money behind violence and be willing to look into the complexities of poverty and corruption – there is a link between violence against women, war and illegal exploitation of minerals (eg coltan) in DR Congo. Most mines in Eastern Congo are controlled by armed militia groups which 'tax' the mines and abuse the population.[6] This money goes to buying weapons which feed the violence and rape. The World Bank has also criticised China for mining deals in the Congo that allowed around $23 million to be paid in bribes.[7]

BREAKOUT Q

- If no one asks the questions, things will never change. Zelophehad's daughters dared to ask questions and the law was changed.
- Beyond the individual stories of women we can see global injustice, involving companies and governments and laws.
- Will you get involved in the campaign against the illegal trade in coltan, a mineral mined in DR Congo that funds violence and death?
- You can find out more at www.w2wglobal.org where the 'Your Call' campaign wants to draw attention to this issue. For further information you can go to www.raisehopeforcongo.org. You can also read more about the plight of women in the Congo at Lynne Hybel's blog: see www.lynnehybels.com

MOVIE EXTRA

Based on real-life events, *Made in Dagenham* follows the story of a group of women working in a huge British Ford factory in 1968. Dissatisfied that they're being paid significantly lower wages than their male counterparts, they set out to achieve a pay increase. But they widen their demands to call for equal pay for equal work. The long struggle that ensues brings heated opposition from union bosses as well as Ford but ultimately the women's advocacy leads to the first legislation on equal pay for work of equal value.

The film shows in a light-hearted way the increasing determination of ordinary women to claim justice and the effect of their strike on their families.

In a scene in the film, one of the principal characters, Rita O'Grady, expressess the attitude of the women workers at Ford:

'Cope? How will we cope? We're women. Now, don't ask such stupid questions.'

BREAKOUT Q

- There are lots of humorous moments in the film, but it shows effective advocacy at work. What methods did the women use that led to success?

NOTES

1 Lifetime risk of maternal mortality in developed nations is 1 in 3,800. See WHO Maternal Mortality factsheet, 2012, http://www.who.int/mediacentre/factsheets/fs348/en/index.html
2 *Ibid.*
3 *Ibid.*
4 You can watch Leymah Gbowee speak at http://www.youtube.com/watch?v=QxkxcsrveLw or visit: www.praythedevilbacktohell.com to find out about the upcoming film telling the story of the women's peace movement in Liberia that ended the second civil war.
5 For more information on the hospital in Goma, see: http://www.healafrica.org
6 From Mine to Mobile, report by the Enough Project, http://www.enoughproject.org/publications/mine-mobile-phone?page=8
7 See http://www.minesandcommunities.org/article.php?a=9924

STUDY 4:
Fighters for justice

CAN WOMEN USE THEIR GIFTS TO RELEASE BLESSING TO PEOPLE CAUGHT IN INJUSTICE?

How can we as women of faith, who know and appreciate God's love and justice, use our capacities to reach other women with good news?

Right now is a wonderful opportunity to call for faith-filled action on poverty. In 2000, at the turn of the new Millennium, leaders in 189 nations made an audacious promise to halve global poverty by 2015. The Millennium Development Goals tackle eight different aspects of extreme poverty and all nations, rich and poor, must do their part to make them happen. As mentioned in Study 2, three of the goals specifically target women and girls: to promote equality and empowerment for women, to reduce child mortality, and to improve maternal health. Each Goal has measurable targets so progress can be assessed.

Widows and girls still lack power and sometimes they are victims. That is why the Goals place particular emphasis upon them. But women are also key to providing solutions. We have an abundance of talent, plus determination to improve life for our families and communities.

BIBLE FOUNDATION

We've seen how women in the Bible – some famous names and some less familiar ones – have faithfully served, led others and been advocates.

Naomi and Ruth are a reminder to us of the way women can encourage and lead. The story is found in the book of Ruth. Naomi, a widow and refugee gives wise advice to her daughter-in-law Ruth which helps restore their economic and social standing. It's also a romance because Ruth finds love and a secure home with Boaz.

But what I love most is that the story recognises that economic and social restoration are linked to hope – Ruth is inspired by Naomi to follow after God, and her marriage to Boaz, a man of faith and integrity, begins the family line that, three generations later, gives Israel King David. Naomi's neighbours are so impressed with Ruth's example that they declare she is better than seven sons (Ruth 4:15)!

Rizpah, concubine to King Saul was a woman who showed great humility and righteousness in mourning her family and in so doing broke a cycle of violence in the land. Her life was marked by famine and violence and she lost seven of her family whose blood was forfeited for the sake of a royal decree.

In 2 Samuel 21:1–14 we learn that Rizpah stays on the mountain where the seven bodies had been left exposed and for months shows her love and grief by protecting them from the vultures by day and the wild animals by night. Eventually, reports of her tenacious fight reach the corridors of power. King David (who had first decreed their deaths) orders the removal of the bodies and, following a proper burial, famine is lifted from the land.

Rizpah's costly vigil is key to this change in David's heart and national policy. The biblical account in 2 Samuel 21 shows that a good leader is a humble leader – someone who prays, listens to the rumours from the periphery, recognises the godly cause in simple acts of righteousness and changes his heart and course in light of this. Rizpah's time of mourning takes place 'under heaven' and is a powerful statement of righteous advocacy on earth. Her actions, in the midst of a cycle of violence, carry something of the eternity that God had placed in her heart (see Ecclesiastes 3:11).

Mary, the mother of Jesus, who lived about 1,000 years after Rizpah and Ruth, also shows us that faith in God can be the key to release us from economic and spiritual poverty. Young, unmarried and pregnant, Mary recognises God's heart for the outsider, for the lowly. Through the baby she carries, she declares that God has 'filled the hungry with good things but has sent the rich empty away' (Luke 1:53).

BREAKOUT Q

- Out of all the biblical women featured in these studies, which one do you most identify with and why?
- Has God released all your potential yet?

VITAL TO KNOW

'Girls who are poor, live in remote areas or belong to minority groups still cannot attend school as easily as boys. Women are more likely than men to work in low-paying occupations, to farm smaller plots and to manage smaller firms in less profitable sectors.

Whether workers, farmers or entrepreneurs, women earn less than men: 20 percent less in Mexico and Egypt; 40 percent less in Georgia, Germany or India; 66 percent less in Ethiopia. Women – especially poor women – have less say over decisions and less control over household resources than men. Women's voice and representation in society, business and politics is significantly lower than men's – with little difference between poor and rich countries.

Leveling the playing field for women would offer huge potential.

Putting resources in the hands of women has been shown to be good not just for them, but also for their children. It increases a child's chances of survival, health and nutrition and school performance.'

Robert Zoellick *(President of the World Bank, 2011[1])*

'Wherever women have the vote, wherever they are literate and have the medical facilities to control the number of children they bear, the birth rate falls.'

Sir David Attenborough *(2011)*

'Women play a crucial role in local economies and the health and well-being of their families. Women who are educated are more likely to have fewer and healthier children. In fact, mothers with some education immunise their children 50 percent more often than mothers who are not educated, while HIV/AIDS spreads twice as quickly among uneducated girls than among girls who have even some schooling.'

CARE International (2005)

'It is impossible to realise our goals (the Millennium Development Goals) while discriminating against half the human race. As study after study has taught us, there is no tool for development more effective than the empowerment of women.'

Kofi Annan (then UN Secretary General, 2006)

BREAKOUT Q

- Do you think these statements are depressing or hopeful?
- Consider what Nicholas Kristof and Sheryl Wudunn have written in their bestselling book, *Half the Sky, How to Change the World* (Virago Press, 2009) about the cruelties inflicted every day on women and girls in poverty:

  'Even when a social problem is so vast as to be insoluble in its entirety, it's still worth mitigating. We may not succeed in educating all the girls in poor countries or in preventing all women from dying in childbirth or in saving all the girls who are imprisoned in brothels. But ... we remember a Hawaiian parable:

  'A man goes out on the beach and sees that it is covered with starfish that have washed up in the tide. A little boy is walking along, picking them up and throwing them back into the water. "What are you doing son?" the man asks. "You see how many starfish there are? You'll never make a difference."

  The boy paused thoughtfully, and picked up another starfish and threw it into the ocean.

  "It sure made a difference to that one," he said.'[2]
- How could you and your group spread the word about inequalities facing women and girls?

LIVES TO INSPIRE

> *'We can do no great things; only small things with great love.'*
>
> ***Mother Teresa** (1910–1997)*

I know lots of women with a deep faith, a breadth of talents and a heart to do something that bit extraordinary for God.

I don't want to call them saints or heroes because that might mean they seem greater than us. The fact is they are simply women prepared to insist that another world is possible. Meet six women – five of whose names I have changed to protect their privacy.

Lyn from Australia is a highly qualified counsellor. After the 2005 Tsunami, she led sessions in Aceh to help pastors counsel grieving families. It was highly unusual for men to be taught by a woman so she helped them to value a female leader.

Cynthia from the UK has been a teacher for twenty-five years in city schools. She gave her holiday time in 2010 and 2011 to train young volunteer teachers, mostly teenage girls, in refugee camps on the Thai/Burma border.

Sophie in Nigeria is a natural leader. Charismatic and bright, in 2010 she brought together women journalists and women factory workers to play a football match to demonstrate how women could overcome differences to tackle poverty and highlight the Millennium Development Goals. The match was televised on national TV.

Jill from Australia inspired women in her church's mums and toddlers group to learn about child deaths in poor communities. They held a fifth birthday party to highlight the issues around child mortality (that many may not reach their fifth birthday) and decorated disposable nappies with the slogan, 'Children are not disposable'. Jill arranged to meet her local member of parliament and presented the nappies to him (they were clean!) asking him to support greater spending for child and maternal health in the aid budget. Her story got in the local paper and has encouraged many other groups to follow the same action.

Patience leads a women's group in a township outside Harare, Zimbabwe. The group was very concerned about the number of women who die in childbirth. There are lots of causes but a main one is the lack of a good clinic in the area. The existing clinic is run-down, dirty and lacking in equipment. The staff are poorly paid and de-motivated.

The women's group decided that they would have a clinic

clean-up. Fifty-four volunteers cleaned wards and corridors, giving special attention to the maternity ward, and also cleared the grounds. Their simple caring action has encouraged the nurses to take greater effort in maintaining the clinic and the head nurse has invited the local pastors into the clinic to pray for the staff and patients. In the past, the nurses have been hostile, fearing criticism, but now they want to work with the church women to save lives. It has also encouraged the women's group to see advocacy as a positive thing, not confrontational.

And finally, a name that hasn't been changed!

In 2002, **Kay Warren**, wife of Rick Warren, pastor and famous author, became, in her words, 'seriously disturbed' by the suffering of the millions infected with or affected by HIV and AIDS. That year she founded the HIV & AIDS Initiative at Saddleback Church. In the last decade, she has spoken at the UN and various Christian gatherings about HIV and is credited with influencing President George W. Bush to support US funding for HIV/AIDs initiatives.

Through the P.E.A.C.E. Plan, she is also campaigning not just on AIDS, but on broader issues of poverty and sound leadership.

PRAYER

Take time to pray – to ask God to show you what could be next for you. Pray for the women who populate the pages of this little book.

ACTION

Could you link up with Woman to Woman?

Woman to Woman is an initiative of Micah Challenge, a campaign to awaken the Church to be a voice for and with the poor so that we can see global poverty halved in our generation.

Be inspired to take up the challenge of changing lives for

women and girls. Keep reading to find lots of ideas that could work in your church, homegroup, classroom or office. We invite you to be committed to reducing economic poverty, committed to empowering girls and women to be change-makers and committed to a biblical model of building families and communities.

MOVIE EXTRA

The Girl in the Café is a romantic comedy with political undertones. When financial advisor to the Chancellor (Treasurer), Lawrence meets the pretty but aimless Gina in a café, he invites her to accompany him to a G8 summit in Reykjavik. Once there she realises that there are issues – such as extreme poverty – about which she has to make a stand, regardless of her social position or possible consequences. She begins offering up advice to the powerful leaders that she runs into at social occasions, although her comments are far from well-received. Her new convictions threaten her relationship with Lawrence.

In the film, Gina insists that 'great decisions' to end poverty are actually easy to make – because it just wouldn't be right to watch kids die and do nothing. For her, poverty and hunger are wrong. Full stop. And inaction is not an option. Her passionate moral argument – 'It must be possible' – made at a formal dinner of world leaders, leaves her audience uncomfortable and ashamed.

BREAKOUT Q

- This film was made specially to highlight the chance that world leaders have to make the Millennium Development Goals a reality. Gina is the voice of compassion. Can compassion work in politics?

NOTES

1 See http://web.worldbank.org/WBSITE/EXTERNAL/COUNTRIES/MENAEXT/0,contentMDK:23004424~menuPK:5649749~pagePK:146736~piPK:146830~theSitePK:256299,00.html

2 Nicholas Kristof and Sheryl WuDunn, *Half the Sky, How to Change the World* (Virago Press: 2009), p.50.

What can I do?

CHALLENGING, INSPIRING, POWERFUL, IMPORTANT – these are just some of the responses I hope you have had to the studies in this book about women's courage, persistence and hope.

You have seen the way God works for and with women in the Bible, you have read stories, watched movies, discussed and prayed. Now it's time to consider more specifically how you could get involved.

How could God use your skills and passions to make a difference for women and girls, especially the powerless?

The most common question I get asked when I speak about a faith-filled response to injustice and suffering is 'What can I do?

And that is why this section is included.

'I realized I had allowed fear to stop me too many times in my life. It was almost like I had two selves, a true self and a fearful self. My true self wanted to shout yes! to the challenges of life. My true self wanted to give, and serve, and make a difference.

'But my fearful self constantly said, "No, no you can't do that. You might fail. You might embarrass yourself. You might disappoint people."'

Lynne Hybels[1]

Don't let fear or timidity, fear of failure or false modesty hold you back.

And don't let life's busy-ness tempt you to think that you have no role in the great issues of our day. Taking action does need time and commitment but it's worth it and remember, we can take small steps:

Elizabeth Fry (see Study 1) had to take the first step to visit the prison, then ask her friends to donate clothes and money. It was only later that she had to be prepared to speak out publicly; Patience and her group (see Study 4) had to plan their clean-up day – liaise with the clinic, find volunteers, involve six different churches and provide all the cleaning materials – but it led to the opportunity to speak out on bigger concerns; Leymah Gbowee (see Study 3) started with an idea to pray. She had to coordinate women from many backgrounds to plan the peace walks. She used imaginative action, media and effective argument – each new opportunity made her bolder – till she was able to present her case at the peace talks.

All of them prayed! All of them stepped beyond their known limits and into God's extraordinary possibilities. And they did it because God called them for 'such a time as this'.

What makes these studies special is the emphasis on advocacy – speaking up and taking public action in support of women and girls in poverty.

You (and your group or church) could do some of these advocacy action ideas:

1. GET ANGRY (TAKE ACTION)

Often, our first reaction to suffering and injustice is to shed tears for those in pain, and feel anger at the perpetrators. Like the psalmists, we should get angry when we see exploitation and cruelty but we should turn our anger into positive action, rather than fretting or fuming. (See, amongst others, Psalms 5; 7; 37.)

Christians are traditionally pretty good at responding to those who are hungry, in prison and naked (or at least we give money to charities that address those needs). But we do less well at turning our anger at injustice into action.

So, get involved with a campaign that aims to stop injustice, eg sign a petition, don't buy products from companies that exploit children or don't pay fair wages, protest against the brothel on the main street of town, don't let your government reject refugees.

In Study 3, you read about Lyn Lusi's work to heal fistulas. A campaign that is trying to stop the appalling violence against women and girls in DR Congo has a number of practical actions that aim to raise awareness, stop the flow of illicit funds to militia groups that perpetrate violence, and link our actions in Sydney or San Francisco to the lives of girls and women in the Congo.

The campaign, 'Your Call', shows how we can help to end the illegal trade in coltan, a mineral used in every mobile phone and laptop. If we clean up the trade, we can protect the lives of women and girls caught in violent conflict in the Congo. See w2wglobal.org and follow the Campaign links.

You can find a variety of campaign ideas in the online resource produced by Micah Challenge – see www.useby2015.org

And remember, don't stay angry – it will just make you bitter or cynical. God wants to turn our anger into action that brings hope.

2. ORGANISE

Organise an event to raise awareness about the issues in these studies. The best way to win people over is with good arguments, evidence, a dose of charm and some passion – just like Esther in the Bible.

You could hold a dinner, have a stall at a community event, run a sporting event or dress up and hand out leaflets at the train station/bus stop. You could also hold a prayer vigil.

You could invite your local politician and other leading community leaders to the event. And get friends and other groups involved – it helps you with the workload and helps overall to show Christianity in a positive light.

3. USE YOUR VOICE (OR FINGERS)

It is an incredible privilege to live in a democracy where we can speak out. We should not leave the public space to professional lobbyists or activists.

Got 20 minutes? Write letters/emails to the government urging just action. We need strong laws to protect trafficked women, people imprisoned for their faith, girls forced into marriage and women who are victims of violent conflict.

Use the same method with business urging action on ethical production, fair wages or sustainable development.

Don't know what to say? There are heaps of examples already out there and as time goes on, you will get more confident.

Groups like Amnesty, and AVAAZ know the value of people taking the time to make their views known to those in authority.

Got 120 minutes? Make an appointment to see your local politician about issues facing women and girls in poverty. Ask their views, clearly express yours. Once you have visited, you will want to do it again!

4. GET NETWORKED

Woman to Woman is a unique venture which has only just got underway. It gives you the opportunity to learn more, to take local action and to be involved in campaigns advocating for justice.

It is an online community with stories (and we'd love to hear your stories), Bible material, prayer ideas, action ideas, poverty information and more.

'Like us' on Facebook, follow our tweets and check out the website – w2wglobal.org

Many denominations have women's networks and you could encourage yours to get involved with advocacy through Woman to Woman.

5. TALK

Chat on Facebook/Twitter and over coffee about issues covered in these studies.

Chat to friends/family about something very practical you could do for women suffering injustice. It may mean raising money for a project that helps girls and women or getting involved in a local project with teenage mums, elderly women or refugees.

Talk about the Bible's views on poverty, injustice and women. Too often, these topics are seen as secondary to prayer and evangelism but the studies should have given you some ammunition against that view!

And there are also the essentials:

PRAY

Pour out your heart to God. When you watch the news or read about an issue of injustice, pray. When you are going to meet up with girlfriends, pray that the time will be more than just a catch-up chat – pray it will be a significant time.

Most of all, tell God about your passion to reach out to women and girls in need and ask Him to show you the next step to take. And remember, God will be alongside you, before you and behind you!

LEARN

It's hard to take effective action and to pray powerfully if you don't know the issues. It's crucial to 'add to your faith … knowledge' (2 Pet. 1:5).

The ideas in these studies don't often reach the news or magazines, and if they do, it's done sensationally. So it can be hard to find information. www.w2w.org tries to keep all the latest news in one place for you to access and the various links will help you dig deeper into the issues if you want. Woman to Woman is also on Facebook and Twitter – share, 'like', retweet – do all you can to spread the word about faith, women and speaking out.

As we learn, we can also pray and talk more effectively. Most of all we become more powerful advocates to stop injustice – research consistently shows that the most powerful weapon against poverty and corruption is education!

ENCOURAGE

Be a mentor to another woman or girl to encourage them to find God's purpose for them and to be active leaders in their community or workplace. Empowered women can be more effective at speaking out and taking action.

It doesn't have to be a formal mentoring programme but all of us should have a mentor and be a mentor at various stages of our lives.

It would be great if you could mentor a teenager at risk or help a person from a different ethnic background – maybe someone who is failing at school, a recent migrant or a single mother. Mentoring at this level builds self-esteem, encourages positive social behaviour, strengthens communication skills, improves school grades and helps the person to set goals.

You can find links to all sorts of resources about mentoring at www.w2wglobal.org

DONATE

Donate time and money to projects for women. If you're not sure what's out there, you can find some global ideas at www. w2wglobal.org. But there are plenty of local initiatives.

At certain times in our lives, we have lots of commitments all piled into twenty-four hours – work, children, church, ageing parents, marriage. If you are super-busy, don't feel guilty about saying no to some requests. At other times of life, we may have much more time. If that's you right now, why not tithe your time to a special project that helps girls and women.

BE A PROPHET FOR THE POOR

Ask church leaders to preach, pray and participate in social justice as an essential part of church life. If there is doubt, give them a copy of *Generous Justice* by Timothy Keller, *On the Side of the Angels* by Joseph D'Souza and Benedict Rogers or *The Politics of Jesus* by John

Howard Yoder. Alternatively you could give them these studies: *Micah's Challenge* or *The Church's Responsibility to the Global Poor* edited by Marijke Hoek and Justin Thacker.

Use charm, a bit of nagging, gossip, song, humour and passion to declare God's heart for women and God's heart for the poor.

Above all, find the things that fit you and go for them. See where God takes you.

Write down your commitments here. Pray and then plan.

WE **CAN** WORK TOGETHER TO INSPIRE CHANGE TO END POVERTY. GOD AND YOU AND I KNOW THEY'RE WORTH IT.

NOTES

1 Lynne Hybels, *Nice Girls Don't Change the World* (Zondervan, 2006) p.91.

Transforming lives

CWR's vision is to enable people to experience personal transformation through applying God's Word to their lives and relationships.

Our Bible-based training and resources help people around the world to:
- Grow in their walk with God
- Understand and apply Scripture to their lives
- Resource themselves and their church
- Develop pastoral care and counselling skills
- Train for leadership
- Strengthen relationships, marriage and family life

and much more.

Our insightful writers provide daily Bible-reading notes and other resources for all ages, and our experienced course designers and presenters have gained an international reputation for excellence and effectiveness.

CWR's Training and Conference Centres in Surrey and East Sussex, England, provide excellent facilities in idyllic settings – ideal for both learning and spiritual refreshment.

CWR **Applying God's Word** *to everyday life and relationships*

CWR, Waverley Abbey House,
Waverley Lane, Farnham,
Surrey GU9 8EP, UK

Telephone: **+44 (0)1252 784700**
Email: **info@cwr.org.uk**
Website: **www.cwr.org.uk**

Registered Charity No 294387
Company Registration No 1990308

Inspiring Women Every Day

Daily Bible-reading notes written by women, for women, to inspire and encourage all ages:

- Increase your faith and ignite your passion for Jesus
- Find practical support to face life's challenges
- Be enlightened by insights into God's Word.

64-page booklet, 120x170mm, published bimonthly
£15.95 UK annual subscription (six issues)
Individual copies: **£2.95 each**

Also available as email subscription/ebook/Kindle

Prices correct at time of printing.